In

The Diary of
Susie King Taylor,
Civil War Nurse

Edited by Margaret Gay Malone
Illustrations by Laszlo Kubinyi

BENCHMARK BOOKS

MARSHALL CAVENDISH
NEW YORK

e: Richard Ritter, Rosemary
strict, teacher-historian-author
Dr. Ben Stark and librarians Pat McGivney, Lucy Cassidy-Van Hoff, Nancy Nicholson,
Carol Nucci, and Derek Leif. Their help has been invaluable.

Benchmark Books
Marshall Cavendish
99 White Plains Road
Tarrytown, New York 10591-9001
www.marshallcavendish.com

Library of Congress Cataloging-in-Publication Data

Taylor, Susie King, b. 1848.
  The diary of Susie King Taylor, Civil War nurse / edited by Margaret Gay Malone.
    p. cm. — (In my own words)
Summary: Excerpts from the diary of a woman who served as nurse to a
regiment of black soldiers fighting for the Union during the Civil War,
including her observations on the treatment of "coloreds" after the war.
Includes bibliographical references and index.
1. Taylor, Susie King, b. 1848—Diaries—Juvenile literature. 2. African American nurses
—Diaries—Juvenile literature. 3. Nurses—United States—Diaries—Juvenile literature.
4. United States—History—Civil War, 1861–1865—Medical care—Juvenile literature.
5. United States—History—Civil War, 1861–1865—Participation, African American—
Juvenile literature. 6. United States—History—Civil War, 1861–1865—Personal narratives
—Juvenile literature. 7. African Americans—Social conditions—To 1964—Juvenile
literature. [1. Taylor, Susie King, b. 1848. 2. Nurses. 3. African Americans—Biography.
4. Women—Biography. 5. United States—History—Civil War, 1861–1865—Participation,
African American. 6. United States—History—Civil War, 1861–1865—Personal narratives.
7. Diaries.] I. Malone, Margaret Gay. II. Title. III. Series.
  E621.T3T39 2003
  973.7'75'092—dc21
                              2003007088
ISBN 0-7614-1648-X

Series design by Adam Mietlowski

Frontispiece and page 9 courtesy of the Manuscripts, Archives & Rare Books Division,
Schomburg Center for Research in Black Culture, the New York Public Library, Astor,
Lenox and Tilden Foundations

Printed in China

1 3 5 6 4 2

To Tom and Michele, with love

REMINISCENCES OF
MY LIFE IN CAMP

WITH THE 33D UNITED STATES
COLORED TROOPS LATE 1ST
S. C. VOLUNTEERS

BY

SUSIE KING TAYLOR

WITH ILLUSTRATIONS

BOSTON
PUBLISHED BY THE AUTHOR
1902

The title page from Susie King Taylor's autobiography, which she published in 1902

Susie's Book

Introduction

Susie King Taylor was born Susie Baker, in the country-side just outside Savannah, Georgia, in 1848. Her mother was a slave in the home of the Grest family. Under Georgia law, because her mother was a slave, Susie was, too. When she was six years old, her owners permitted her and her younger sister and brother to live with their grandmother Dolly Reed in Savannah.

Savannah was a busy city, known for its luxurious homes and flower-filled squares. Life in the city gave the young girl the opportunity to learn reading and writing at a neighbor's secret school for black children. Because education was forbidden to black people in Georgia, any-one who taught them could have been whipped and fined.

Susie was thirteen when the Civil War began in April 1861. A year later, as fierce fighting "jarred the earth" around Savannah, she was sent back to her moth-er in the country. Then the Yankees captured Fort Pulaski in Savannah Harbor. Susie fled the city with her family and soon made her way to Saint Simons Island, off the coast of southern Georgia. White plantation owners had evacuated the island, leaving behind a small popula-tion of slaves to work the fields. That population grew to include hundreds of black families who came to the island seeking the protection of the Union ships that patrolled along the Georgia coast.

In 1862 Susie married Edward King, a sergeant in the First South Carolina Volunteers, the first black regiment in the Union army. Because she was hired to do the soldiers' laundry, she was permitted to travel with the troops. Susie followed her husband's regiment along the southeastern Atlantic coast, staying on several of the Sea Islands that dot the coastline of South Carolina, Georgia, and northern Florida. She not only washed the men's clothes but also cooked for them, taught them to read and write, and nursed the wounded after battles.

Susie King lived in exciting and dangerous times. During the war, 2,700 black soldiers were killed in action, and Susie often worked close to the battlefields where they fought. Several times Union officers moved her away from the fighting for her own safety. She was with the black troops when they first heard the Emancipation Proclamation, the order issued by President Abraham Lincoln freeing the slaves. Susie celebrated with them on that day, which she called "glorious."

Susie King's life was very different after the war. Shortly after it ended, her husband died, just before their son was born. Susie struggled to support her child, working as a teacher, cook, and laundress. In 1874 she moved to Boston, where she found work as a housekeeper with a well-to-do family.

Although the Civil War had resulted in emancipation, the four million freed slaves were far from truly free. In

Susie was a dedicated nurse and educator, who often risked her life to help the "boys" in her regiment.

the dozen years following the war—the period called Reconstruction—whites continued to oppress blacks, especially in the South. State governments passed laws known as black codes, which restricted the rights of the former slaves. The codes limited the rights of blacks to work and own land and provided for segregation in public places. Poor black families, unable to buy their own land, often ended up as tenant farmers, or sharecroppers, on land owned by whites. Because they were underpaid for their crops and overcharged for clothing and other supplies, they fell deeper into debt as time went on. The terrorist activities of the Ku Klux Klan and other "white supremacy" groups kept them from voting.

At the same time, black people made a number of strides during Reconstruction. Many former slaves reunited their families and gained an education. Three amendments to the Constitution went a long way toward providing equal rights to African Americans. The Thirteenth Amendment, ratified in 1865, guaranteed their freedom. The Fourteenth Amendment made them citizens and provided equal protection under the law, and the Fifteenth Amendment gave black men the right to vote. (Women, black and white, would not gain the vote until the Nineteenth Amendment was passed in 1920.) Increasingly, African Americans ran for office, acquired land and businesses, and began the long struggle toward full equality.

Living in Boston, Susie King escaped the worst of the injustices suffered by Southern blacks during Reconstruction. She was troubled by the news from the South, however, and experienced prejudice firsthand on a visit to her son in Louisiana. During her journey through the South, she was forced to ride in the train's filthy, run-down "colored people's coach," and along the way she saw and heard of blacks who were "murdered in cold blood for nothing."

Susie was especially outraged by the treatment of black veterans in both the North and the South. She knew how bravely these men had fought in the Civil War, and she believed that the country should recognize their contributions. She worked hard organizing a women's group to provide the veterans with "comfort in the twilight of their lives."

In 1879 Susie King married Russell Taylor. In 1902, ten years before her death, she published her autobiography. This is the story of the important events in her life, told in her own words.

—Margaret Gay Malone
Sea Cliff, New York

Selections from the

autobiography of Susie King Taylor,

former slave, Civil War nurse, laundress, cook, and teacher,

published by herself and telling of her life in camp

with the 33rd U.S. Colored Troops

My Childhood

I was born under the slave law in Georgia, in 1848, and was brought up by my grandmother in Savannah. There were three of us with her, my younger sister and brother and I. We were sent to a friend of my grandmother, Mrs. Woodhouse, to learn to read and write. She was a free woman and lived on Bay Lane, about half a mile from my house. We went every day about nine o'clock, with our books wrapped in paper to prevent the police or white persons from seeing them. We went in, one at a time, through the gate, into the yard to the kitchen, which was the schoolroom. She had twenty-five or thirty children whom she taught, assisted by her daughter, Mary Jane.

The neighbors would see us going in sometimes, but they supposed we were there learning trades, as it was the custom to give children a trade of some kind. After school we left the same way we entered, one by one. About a block from the school, we would wait for each other. On our way home we would gather laurel leaves and pop them on our hands.

I remained at Mrs. Woodhouse's school for two years or more, when I was sent to a Mrs. Mary Beasley. I continued there until May 1860, when she told my grand-mother she had taught me all she knew, and Grandmother had better get someone else who could teach me more, so I stopped my studies for a while.

I had a white playmate about this time, named Katie O'Connor, who lived on the next corner of the street from my house, and who attended a convent. One day she told me, if I would promise not to tell her father, she would give me some lessons. On my promise not to do so, and getting her mother's consent, she gave me lessons for about four months, every evening. At the end of this time she was put into the convent permanently, and I have never seen her since.

A month after this, James Blouis, our landlord's son, was attending the high school, so Grandmother asked him to give me a few lessons. He did until the middle of 1861.

I often wrote passes for my grandmother. All colored persons, free or slaves, were compelled to have a pass; free colored people had a guardian in place of a master. These passes were good until 10 or 10:30 P.M. for one month. Every person had to have this pass, for at nine o'clock each night a bell was rung, and any colored persons found on the street after this hour were arrested by the watch-man and put in the guardhouse. The next morning, their owners would pay their fines and release them. I knew a

All colored persons, free or slaves, were compelled to have a pass.

number of persons who went out at any time at night and were never arrested. The watchman knew them so well he never stopped them, and seldom asked to see their passes. Sometimes he would say "Howdy," and then tell them to go along.

About this time I had been reading so much about the "Yankees" that I was very anxious to see them. The whites would tell their colored people not to go to the Yankees, saying they would harness them to carts and make them pull the carts around in place of horses. I asked Grandmother one day if this was true. She replied, "Certainly not!" The white people did not want slaves to go over to the Yankees, and told them these things to frighten them. I wanted to see these wonderful Yankees so much, as I heard my parents say the Yankee was going to set all the slaves free. Oh, how these people prayed for freedom!

I Become a Teacher

On April 1, 1862, about the time the Union soldiers were firing on Fort Pulaski [just east of Savannah], I was sent out into the country to my mother. I remember what a roar and din the guns made. They jarred the earth for miles. At last, the fort fell to the Yankees, and two days later my uncle took his family of seven and myself to Saint Catherine Island. We landed under the protection of the Union fleet, and remained there two weeks, when about thirty of us were taken aboard a gunboat and transferred to Saint Simons Island.

After we were all settled aboard and started on our journey, Captain Whitmore, commanding the boat, asked me if I could read. I said, "Yes!" "Can you write?" he asked next. "Yes, I can do that also," I replied. As if he had some doubts, he handed me a book and a pencil and told me to write my name and where I was from. I did that. Then he wanted to know if I could sew. On hearing I could, he asked me to hem some napkins for him.

After I had been on Saint Simons about three days, Commodore Goldsborough heard of me, and came to see me. He said Captain Whitmore had spoken about me, and that he was pleased to hear of my being so capable. He asked me to take charge of a school for the children on the island. I told him I would gladly do so, if I could have some books. He said I should have them, and in a week or two I received two large boxes of books and Bibles from the North. I had about forty children to teach, besides a number of adults who came to me nights, all of them so eager to learn to read, above anything else.

There were about six hundred colored men, women, and children on Saint Simons, the women and children being in the majority. We were afraid to go very far from

THE FIRST BLACK REGIMENT

The year 1862 marked a dramatic change in the Union army. For the first time since the Civil War began, blacks were enlisted, armed, and allowed to fight. Black men had fought in the American Revolution, but a federal law passed in 1792 had barred them from further service in state militias or the U.S. Army. Now, after a year of war, the North needed more troops, but many whites still opposed arming black men. Abolitionists—people who supported the abolition, or end, of slavery—led the campaign for black enlistment.

In July 1862 Congress changed the law to allow blacks to fight. General Rufus Saxton, military governor of the South Carolina Sea Islands, was authorized to raise five regiments of black soldiers. In November the First South Carolina Volunteer Regiment was sworn into service, becoming the first black regiment officially authorized by the federal government. Abolitionist Thomas Wentworth Higginson became the regiment's commander. Captain Charles T. Trowbridge, who had helped organized the regiment, commanded one of its companies. When Higginson retired in 1864 because of war injuries, Trowbridge took command of the First South Carolina Volunteers.

our own quarters in the daytime, and at night even to go out of the house for a long time. Although the men were on the watch all the time, there were not any soldiers on the island, only the marines who were on the gunboats along the coast. The rebels [Confederate soldiers], knowing this, could steal by them under cover of the night. Getting on the island, they would capture any persons venturing out alone. Several of the men disappeared and were never heard from.

The latter part of August 1862, Captain C. T. Trowbridge, with his brother John and Lieutenant Walker, came to Saint Simons Island from Hilton Head. He was under orders to get all the men possible to finish filling his regiment, which he had organized some months before. He found me teaching at my little school and was much interested in it. When I knew him better, I found him to be a thorough gentleman and a staunch friend to my race.

Life in Camp

Captain Trowbridge remained with us until October, when the order was received to evacuate. We boarded the *Ben-De-Ford*, a transport, for Beaufort, South Carolina. When we arrived in Beaufort, Captain Trowbridge and the men he had enlisted went to camp at Old Fort, which they named Camp Saxton. I was enrolled as laundress.

The first suits worn by the boys were red coats and pants, which they disliked very much, for they said, "The rebels see us miles away."

The first colored troops did not receive any pay for eighteen months. The men had to depend on what they received from the commissary,* established by General Saxton. A great many of these men had large families. As they had no money to give them, their wives were obliged to support themselves and their children. The women did washing for the officers of the gunboats and the soldiers, and made cakes and pies which they sold to the boys in camp. Finally, in 1863, the government decided to give the soldiers half pay, but the men would not accept this. They wanted full pay or nothing. They preferred to give

*commissary—a store with food and supplies for those in the military

22

their services to the state, which they did until 1864, when the government granted them full pay, with all the back pay due.

I remember hearing Captain Alexander Heasley of Company E telling his men one day, "Boys, stand up for your full pay! I am with you, and so are all the officers."

I had a number of relatives in this regiment—several uncles, some cousins, and a husband in Company E, and a number of cousins in other companies.

In February 1863, several cases of varioloid [a form of the contagious disease smallpox] broke out among the boys, which caused some anxiety in camp. Edward Davis of Company E (the company I was with) had it very badly. He was put into a tent apart from the rest of the men, and only the doctor was allowed to see or attend him; but I went to see this man every day and nursed him. The last thing at night, I always went in to see that he was comfortable, but in spite of the good care and attention he received, he died of the disease.

I was not the least afraid of the smallpox. I had been vaccinated, and I drank sassafras tea constantly, which kept my blood clean and prevented me from contracting this dread scourge. No one need fear getting it if they keep their blood in good condition with this sassafras tea, and take it before going where the patient is.

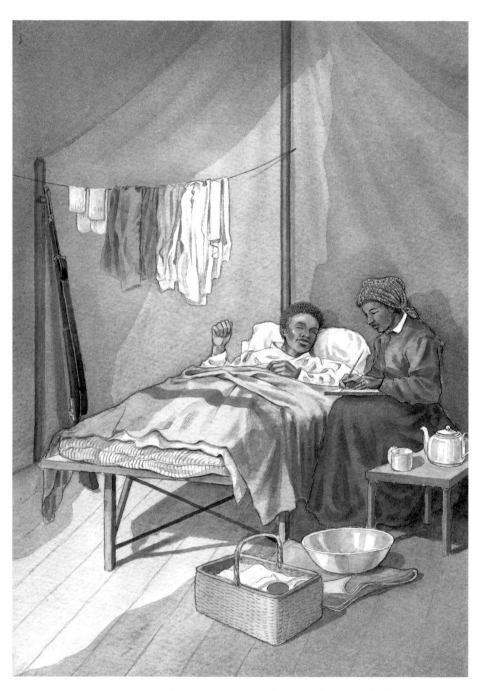

I went to see this man every day and nursed him.

SMALLPOX AND SASSAFRAS TEA

Susie's belief that sassafras tea prevented her from contracting smallpox, a contagious and sometimes fatal disease, was typical of the many mistaken ideas about health and medicine in Civil War times. Actually, it was probably the fact that she had been vaccinated that protected her from the disease. Large numbers of soldiers and those who traveled with them were vaccinated against smallpox. Through a scratch on the skin, they were given a tiny dose of the disease so that their bodies could develop protection against a more serious infection.

Smallpox killed fewer Civil War soldiers than other diseases such as pneumonia, typhoid, malaria, and dysentery (severe diarrhea). Poor nutrition and poor hygiene contributed to disease among the troops. Soldiers often had to eat spoiled meat and drink contaminated water. Latrines (outdoor toilets) were set up too close to where they ate and slept. The men often went for months without a bath or a change of clothes and slept out in the rain and cold. Because of these miserable conditions, twice as many soldiers died from disease as from battle wounds.

A Grand Barbecue

On the first of January, 1863, we held services to listen to the reading of President Lincoln's Emancipation Proclamation by Dr. W. H. Brisbane, and the presentation of two beautiful stands of colors.* It was a glorious day for us all. We enjoyed every minute of it, and as a fitting close and the crowning event of this occasion we had a grand barbecue. A number of oxen were roasted whole, and we had a fine feast. Although not served as tastily or correctly as it would have been at home, yet it was enjoyed with keen appetites. The soldiers had a good time. They sang or shouted "Hurrah!" all through the camp, and seemed overflowing with fun and frolic until taps were sounded, when many, no doubt, dreamt of this memorable day.

*stands of colors —groups of flags

Military Expeditions

March 10, 1863, we were ordered to Jacksonville, Florida. Leaving Camp Saxton between four and five o'clock, we sailed down the coast, arriving at Jacksonville about eight o'clock the next morning. Three or four gunboats accompanied us. When the rebels saw these boats, they ran out of the city, leaving the women behind. We found out afterward that they thought we had a much larger fleet than we really had. The men in our regiment were kept out of sight until our boats made fast at the wharf.

As our men disembarked and began to march up the street, our gunboats helped provide cover by shelling up the river and as far inland as possible. It wasn't long before our group spied the rebels who had fled the city. They were hiding behind a house about a mile or so away, their faces blackened to disguise themselves as Negroes. Our boys, as they advanced toward them, halted a second, saying, "They are black men! Let them come to us, or we will make them know who we are." With this, the firing began, and several of our men were wounded and killed. The rebels had a number wounded and killed. That is

"They are black men! Let them come to us, or we will make
them know who we are."

how we discovered that they were white men. Our men drove them some distance in retreat.

While the fighting was on, a friend, Lizzie Lancaster, and I stopped at several of the rebel homes. After talking with some of the women and children, we asked them if they had any food. They claimed to have only some hard-tack, and evidently did not care to give us anything to eat, but this was not surprising. They were bitterly against our people and had no mercy or sympathy for us.

The second day, our boys were reinforced by a regiment of white soldiers—a Maine regiment—and by cavalry, and they had quite a fight. The third day, there was another battle, which lasted several hours, until the Union boys succeeded in driving the enemy back.

A Rebel Trick

After this battle, every afternoon between four and five o'clock, the Confederate General Finegan would send a flag of truce to Colonel Higginson. General Finegan kept sending these communications for nearly a week. Then Colonel Higginson's headquarters took a direct hit. The shelling was so heavy that the colonel told my captain to take me up into the town to a hotel, which was used as a hospital. I expected every moment to be killed by a shell, but on arriving at the hospital I knew I was safe, for the shells could not reach us there. It was plain to see that the flag of truce coming so often to us was a ruse. The bearer was evidently a spy whose intention was to get the location of the headquarters, for the shells were sent too accurately to be at random.

The next morning Colonel Higginson took our men on another tramp after the rebels. They were gone several days and had the hardest fight they had had. Our boys returned with only a few killed and wounded, and after this we were not troubled with General Finegan.

The Rebs across the River

Several weeks later, our company was ordered to Barnwell plantation [on Barnwell's Island in South Carolina] for picket duty.* Some mornings I would go along the picket line, and I could see the rebels on the opposite side of the river. Sometimes as they were changing pickets they would call over to our men and ask for something to eat, or for tobacco, and our men would tell them to come over. Sometimes one or two would desert to us. Others would shoot across at our picket. But as the river was so wide, there never was any damage done, and the Confederates never attempted to shell us while we were there.

*picket duty—standing guard to prevent a surprise attack

30

I learned to handle a musket very well while in the regiment, and could shoot straight and often hit the target. Each day I assisted in cleaning the guns and used to fire them off to see if the cartridges were dry before cleaning and reloading them. I thought this great fun. I was also able to take a gun all apart and put it back together again.

A Spy Is Shot

While the regiment was at Camp Shaw, near Beaufort, South Carolina, a deserter from the Union army came into town. He was allowed his freedom about the city. He remained for a little while and then returned to the rebels. When he made his appearance in Beaufort a second time, he was held as a spy, tried, and sentenced to death, for he was a traitor. The day he was to be shot, he was placed on a hearse with his coffin inside. He was driven through town with a guard on either side of the hearse. All the soldiers and people in the town were out, as this was to be a warning to the soldiers. Our regiment was in line on dress parade. They drove with him to the rear of our camp, where he was shot. I shall never forget this scene.

While we were at the camp, the rebels captured Chaplain Fowler, Robert Defoe, and several of our boys, who were tapping some telegraph wires. Robert Defoe was confined in the jail at Walterborough, South Carolina, for about twenty months. When [Union General William T.] Sherman's army reached Pocotaligo, South Carolina, he made his escape and rejoined his company. He had not been paid, as he had refused the reduced pay offered to colored troops by the government. But before the payrolls were finally made out, he contracted smallpox and died. He was buried at Savannah, never having been paid one cent for nearly three years of service. He left no heirs and his account was never settled.

Keeping Warm and Well Fed

In winter, when it was very cold, I would take a mess pan, put a little earth in the bottom, go to the cookshed and fill the pan nearly full of coals, and carry it back to my tent. I put another pan over it so that when the guards went through camp after taps, they would not see the light. (It was against the rules to have a light after taps.) In this way I was heated and kept very warm.

I often got my own meals, and would fix some dishes for the non-commissioned officers also. We had fresh beef once in a while, though salt beef was our standby. And we would have soup. The vegetables they put in this soup were dried and pressed. Sometimes the men

The Soldiers' Diet

Union soldiers ate hardtack almost every day. This was a square or rectangular biscuit with small holes in it, which looked like a large soda cracker. The biscuits were baked in Northern factories, and it usually took months for them to reach the troops in the field. By then, they were very hard. Soldiers ate their hardtack plain or crumbled it into fried pork to make a dish called skillygallee.

Besides this staple food, Union soldiers ate meat that was preserved through salting, such as salt pork and salt beef, or smoking, such as bacon. Their meals also included dried or canned fruits and vegetables. Sugar and salt were added to give some flavor to this bland diet.

would have what we called slapjacks. This was flour, made into a batter and spread thin on the bottom of the mess pan to cook. Each man would have one of these pancakes with a pint of tea for his supper, or a pint of tea and five or six hardtack.

Caring for the "Boys"

Mrs. Chamberlain, our quartermaster's wife, was with us here [at Camp Shaw]. She was a beautiful woman. I can see her pleasant face before me now, as she, with Captain Trowbridge, would sit and converse with me in my tent two or three hours at a time. I remember how, when she first came into camp, Captain Trowbridge brought her to my tent and introduced her to me. I found her then, as she remained ever after, a lovely person, and I always admired her cordial and friendly ways.

Soldiers from other companies would say to me sometimes, "Mrs. King, why is it you are so kind to us? You treat us just as you do the boys in your own company." I replied, "Well, you know, all the boys in other companies are the same to me as those in my Company E. You are all doing the same duty, and I will do just the same for you." "Yes," they would say, "we know that, because you were the first woman we saw when we came into camp, and you took an interest in us boys ever since we have been here, and we are very grateful for all you do for us."

When at Camp Shaw, I visited the hospital in Beaufort, where I met Clara Barton. There were a number of sick and wounded soldiers there, and I went often to see the comrades. Miss Barton was always very cordial toward me, and I honored her for her devotion and care of those men.

War's Gruesome Sights

The regiment was ordered to Morris Island [in Charleston Harbor] between June and July 1864. Because Fort Wagner was only a mile from our camp, I went there two or three times a week. I would go up on the ramparts to watch the gunners send their shells into Charleston. Outside of the fort were many skulls lying about. I often moved them out of the path. The comrades and I would have quite a debate as to which side those men had fought on. Some thought they were the skulls of our boys. Others thought they were the enemy's. There was no definite way to know, and it was never decided who could lay claim to them. They were a gruesome sight, those fleshless heads and grinning jaws, but by this time I had become accustomed to worse things and did not feel as I might have earlier in my camp life.

It seems strange how our aversion to seeing suffering is overcome in war. We are able to see the most sickening sights, such as men with their limbs blown off and mangled by the deadly shells, without a

THE ANGEL OF THE BATTLEFIELD

Helping others was Clara Barton's mission in life. Barton was born in Massachusetts on Christmas Day 1821. An intelligent and dedicated young woman, she taught school for eighteen years. When the Civil War broke out, she advertised for donations of bandages, socks, and other supplies for the Union troops and set up an agency to distribute them. A year later, she received the government's permission to personally deliver supplies and nurse the sick and wounded at the battlefront. In 1864 Clara Barton was appointed superintendent of all Union nurses. For her devotion to the soldiers, she was nicknamed the Angel of the Battlefield. Today she is best known as the founder of the American Red Cross.

shudder. Instead of turning away, how we hurry to assist in alleviating their pain, bind up their wounds, and press cool water to their parched lips, with feelings only of sympathy and pity.

The Assault on Fort Gregg

The regiment had troublesome times from Fort Gregg, on James Island [in Charleston Harbor], for the rebels would throw a shell over on our island every now and then. Finally orders were received for the boys to prepare to assault Fort Gregg, each man to take 150 rounds of cartridges, canteens of water, hardtack, and salt beef. This order was sent three days prior to starting, to allow them to be in readiness.

The fourth day, about five o'clock in the afternoon on July 1, 1864, the call was sounded, and I heard the first sergeant say, "Fall in, boys, fall in," and they were not long obeying the command. Each company marched out. The line was formed with the 103rd New York (a white regiment) in the rear, and off they started, eager to get to work. I have never forgotten the good-byes of that day as they left camp. Colonel Trowbridge said to me, "Good-bye, Mrs. King, take care of yourself if you don't see us again." I went with them as far as the landing, and watched them until they got out of sight, and then I returned to the camp. There was no one at camp but those left on picket and a few disabled soldiers, and one woman, a friend of mine, Mary Shaw. It was lonesome and sad, now that the boys were gone, some never to return.

About four o'clock, July 2, the charge on Fort Gregg was made. The firing could be plainly heard in camp. I hastened down to the landing and remained there until eight o'clock that morning. When the wounded began to arrive, the first one brought in was Samuel Anderson of our company. He was badly wounded. Then came others of our boys, some with their legs off, arm gone, foot off, and wounds of all kinds imaginable. They had been forced to wade through creeks and marshes, as they were discovered by the enemy and shelled very badly. A number of the men were lost. Some got fastened in the mud and had to cut off the legs of their pants to free themselves. The 103rd New York suffered the most as their men were very badly wounded.

My work now began. I gave my assistance to try to alleviate the men's sufferings. I asked the doctor at the hospital what I could get for them to eat. They wanted soup, but that I could not get. I had a few cans of condensed milk and some turtle eggs, so I thought I would try to make some custard. I had doubts as to my success, for cooking with turtle eggs was something new to me. But the adage has it, "Nothing ventured, nothing done," so I made a venture, and the result was a very delicious custard. This I carried to the men, who enjoyed it very much.

My services were given at all times for the comfort of these men. I was on hand to assist whenever needed. I was enrolled as company laundress, but I did very little washing, because I was always busy doing other things for the officers and comrades.

After this fight, the regiment did not return to the camp for one month. The rebels found out that some of our forces had been removed and gave our boys in camp a hard time of it for several nights. In fact, one night it was thought the boys would have to retreat. The colonel told me that if they were obliged to retreat, I should go down to the landing and climb aboard a gunboat to escape. As it turned out, one of our gunboats began to shell [Confederate] General Beauregard's force, which helped our boys hold their position.

A Pet Pig

I must mention a pet pig we had on one of the islands. One day, Colonel Trowbridge brought into camp a poor, thin little pig, which a soldier had brought back with him on his return from a furlough. The man's regiment, the 74th Pennsylvania, was just embarking for the North, and

So well did the drummer boys train him that, every day at practice and dress parade, his pigship would march out with them, keeping perfect time with their music.

he could not take the pig back with him, so he gave it to our colonel. That pig grew to be the pet of the camp, and was the special care of the drummer boys, who taught him many tricks. So well did they train him that every day at practice and dress parade, his pigship would march out with them, keeping perfect time with their music.

A Disastrous Journey

Around November 15, 1864, I received a letter from my husband, saying the boys were lying three miles from Gregg Landing, South Carolina, and had not had another fight yet, but the rebels were waiting for them. After receiving this letter, I wanted to get to Beaufort, so I could be near to them and be able to get news from my husband.

There was a large sailboat that carried passengers to Beaufort. The only people here, besides the soldiers, were Mrs. Lizzie Brown, who came over with a permit to see her husband, who was very ill; Corporal Walker's wife, with her two-year-old child; and Mrs. Seabrooke. As soon as we could get the boat, we took passage for Beaufort. It was nearly dark before we had gone any distance, and about eight o'clock the boat overturned. We were cast away and were only saved through the mercy of God. I remember going down twice. As I rose the second time, I caught hold of the sail and managed to hold some part of the boat. We drifted and shouted as loud as we could, trying to attract the attention of some of the government boats on the river. It was in vain; we could not make ourselves heard.

Just when we gave up all hope, and in the last moment gave one more despairing cry, we were heard at Ladies' Island. Two boats were launched and a search was made to locate us. They found us at last, nearly dead from exposure. In fact, the poor little child was dead, although Mrs. Walker still held her by her clothing, with her teeth. I had to be carried, as I was thoroughly exhausted. We were given the best attention we could get at the place where we were picked up.

The men who saved us were surprised when they found me among the passengers, as one of them, William Geary, of Darien, Georgia, was a friend of my husband. Mr. Geary's mother lived about two miles from where we were picked up. She told me she had heard cries for a long time that night and had been very uneasy about it.

Finally she said to her son, "I think some poor souls are cast away."

"I don't think so, Mother," he replied. "I saw some people going down the river today. You know this is Christmas, and they are having a good time."

But she still persisted that these were cries of distress,

and not of joy, and begged him to go out and see. To satisfy her, he went outside and listened. Then he heard the cries also, and hastened to get the boats off to find us. We were capsized about 8:15 P.M., and it was near midnight when they found us. Next day, they kept a sharp lookout on the beach for anything that might have washed in from the boat. They retrieved a trunk and several other things.

I was very ill and under the doctor's care for some time in Beaufort. I had swallowed a lot of water. In January 1865, I went back to Cole Island, where I could be attended by my doctor, Dr. Miner. He did all in his power to alleviate my suffering, for I was swollen very much. This he reduced and I recovered, but had a severe cough for a long time afterward.

The Final Days of War

In October 1864, six companies of the regiment were ordered to Gregg Landing, on a river in South Carolina. In some way our mail had been sent over to the Confederate side and their mail to us. Captain Metcalf and Lieutenant West were detailed to exchange these letters under a flag of truce. So, with an escort of six men, the flag was unfurled and a message shouted across the river to the Confederates.

Captain Metcalf asked them to come over to our side under the protection of our flag of truce. The Confederates refused. As an excuse they said their boat was too far up the river and so they had no way to cross the river to us. They asked Metcalf to cross to them. He at once ordered his men to "stack arms,"* the Confederates following suit. His boys in blue rowed him over, and he introduced himself to the rebel officers.

One of these officers was Major Jones of Alabama, the other Lieutenant Scott of South Carolina. Major Jones was very cordial to our captain, but Lieutenant Scott would not extend his hand, and stood aside in sullen silence.

*stack arms—put down weapons

Major Jones said to Captain Metcalf, "Should I meet you again, I shall not forget we have met before." With this he extended his hand to Metcalf and bade him good-bye, but Lieutenant Scott stood by and looked as cross as he possibly could. The letters were exchanged, but it seemed a mystery just how those letters got missent to the opposite sides. Captain Metcalf said he did not feel a mite comfortable while he was on the Confederate soil. As for his men, you can imagine their thoughts.

I asked them how they felt on the other side, and they said, "We would have felt much better if we had had our guns with us." It was a little risky, for sometimes the flag of truce is not regarded, but even among the enemy there are some good and loyal persons.

Charleston Is Captured

On February 28, 1865, the remainder of the regiment were ordered to Charleston, South Carolina, as there were signs of the rebels evacuating that city. We arrived in Charleston between nine and ten o'clock in the morning, and found the rebs had set fire to the city and fled, leaving women and children behind to suffer and perish in the flames. The fire had been burning fiercely for a day and night. When we landed, under a flag of truce, our regiment went to work assisting the citizens in putting

Major Jones was very cordial to our captain, but Lieutenant Scott would not extend his hand and stood aside in sullen silence.

out the flames. It was a terrible scene. For three or four days the men fought the fire. They saved the property and effects of the people, yet these white men and women could not tolerate our black Union soldiers, for many of them had formerly been their slaves. Although these brave men risked life and limb to assist them in their distress, men and even women would sneer and molest them whenever they met them.

I had quarters assigned me at a residence on South Battery Street, one of the most aristocratic parts of the city, where I assisted in caring for the sick and injured comrades. After getting the fire under control, the regiment marched out to the racetrack, where they camped until March 12, when we were ordered to Savannah, Georgia. We arrived there on the thirteenth, about eight o'clock in the evening, and marched out to Fairlong, where we remained about ten days. We were ordered to Augusta, Georgia, where our captain, Alexander Heasley, was shot and killed by a Confederate. After his death Lieutenant Parker was made captain of the company, and he was with us until the regiment was mustered out. He often told me about his home state, Massachusetts, but I had no thought at that time that I would ever live there and stand in the "Cradle of Liberty."

The regiment remained in Augusta for thirty days,

when it was ordered to Hamburg, South Carolina, and then on to Charleston. It was while on their march through the country that the men came in contact with the bushwhackers (as the rebels were called). They hid in the bushes and would shoot the Union boys every chance they got. Other times they would conceal themselves in the railroad cars used to transfer our soldiers. When our boys, worn out and tired, would fall asleep, these men would come out from their hiding places and cut their throats. Several of our men were killed in this way, but it could not be found out who was committing these murders until one night one of the rebels was caught in the act, trying to cut the throat of a sleeping soldier. He was put under guard, court-martialed, and shot.

Mustered Out

On February 9, 1866, "General Orders" were received and the regiment mustered out. The men were delighted to go home, but oh! How they hated to part from their commanding chief, Colonel C. T. Trowbridge. He was the very first officer to take charge of black soldiers. We thought there was no one like him, for he was a "man" among his soldiers. All in the regiment knew him personally, and many were the jokes he used to tell them. I shall never forget his friendship and kindness toward me, from the first time I met him to the end of the war. If anyone from the North came into our camp, he would bring them to see me.

While on a visit South in 1888, I met a comrade of the regiment, who often said to me, "You up North, Mrs. King, do you ever see Colonel Trowbridge? How I should like to see him! I don't see why he does not come South sometime. Why, I would take a day off and look up all the 'boys' I could find, if I knew he was coming."

I knew this man meant what he said, for the men of the regiment knew Colonel Trowbridge first of all the other officers. He was with them on Saint Simons Island and at Camp Saxton. I remember when the company was being formed, we wished Captain C. T. was our captain, because most of the men in Company E were the men he brought with him from Saint Simons, and they were attached to him. He was always jolly and pleasing with all. No officer in the army was more beloved than our lieutenant colonel, C. T. Trowbridge.

Let Us Remember

My dear friends! Do we understand the meaning of war? Do we know or think of that war of '61? No, we do not. Only those brave soldiers, and those who had occasion to be in it, can realize what it was. I can never forget that terrible war until my eyes close in death. The scenes are just as fresh in my mind today as in '61. I see now each scene—the roll call, the drum tap, lights out, the call at night when there was danger from the enemy, the pickets, the cold and rain. How anxious I would be, not knowing what would happen before morning! Many times I would dress, not sure but all would be captured. Other times I would stand at my tent door and try to see what was going on, because night was the time the rebels would try to get into our lines and capture some of the boys. It was mostly at night that our men went out looking for Confederate scouts, and often had a hand-to-hand fight with the rebels.

We do not, as the black race, properly appreciate the old veterans, white or black, as we ought to. I know what they went through, especially those black men. The Confederates had no mercy on them; neither did they show any toward the white Union soldiers. I have seen the terrors of that war. I was the wife of one of those men who did not get a penny for eighteen months for their services, only their rations and clothing.

I look around now and see the comforts that our younger generation enjoy, and think of the blood that was shed to make these comforts possible for them, and see how little some of them appreciate the old soldiers. My heart burns within me, at this want of appreciation. There are only a few of them left now, so let us all, as the ranks close, take a deeper interest in them.

There are many people who do not know what some of the colored women did during the war. There were hundreds of them who assisted the Union soldiers who escaped from Confederate prisons, hiding them and helping them to make their way back to safety. Many women were punished for taking food to the prison stockades for the prisoners. When I went into Savannah in 1865, I was told of one of these stockades in the suburbs of the city, and they said it was an awful place. The colored women would take food there at night and pass it to the prisoners through the holes in the fence.

The soldiers were starving, and these women did all they could to relieve those men, although they knew the penalty should they be caught. Others assisted the Union army in various ways. These things should be kept in history before the people. There has never been a greater war in the United States than the one in 1861, where so many lives were lost, not men alone but noble women as well.

A New Life

At the close of the war, my husband and I returned to Savannah. A new life was before us now, all the old life left behind. After getting settled, I opened a school at my home on South Broad Street, now called Oglethorpe Avenue, as there was not any public school for Negro children. I had twenty children at my school, and received one dollar a month for each pupil. I also had a few older ones who came at night. I taught almost a year, when the Beach Institute opened, which took a number of my scholars, as it was a free school.

Sergeant King, my husband, was a boss carpenter. Just mustered out of the army, and the prejudice against his race still too strong to ensure him much work at his trade, he took contracts for unloading vessels, and hired a number of men to assist him. He was much respected by the citizens and was a favorite with his associates. On September 16, 1866, Sergeant King died, leaving me soon to welcome a little stranger, our baby son, alone.

In December 1866 I was obliged to give up teaching, but in April 1867 I opened a school in Liberty County,

Georgia, and taught there one year. Country life did not agree with me, so I returned to the city, and Mrs. Susie Carrier took charge of my school.

On my return to Savannah, I found that the free school had taken all my former pupils, so I opened a night school, where I taught a number of adults. This, together with other things I could get to do and the assistance of my brother-in-law, supported me. I taught this school until the fall of 1868, when a free night school opened at the Beach Institute, and again my scholars left me to attend this free school. So I had to close my school. I put my baby with my mother and entered into the employ of a family, where I lived quite a while, but had to leave, as the work was too hard.

I Move to the North

In 1872 I put in a claim for my husband's bounty and received one hundred dollars, some of which I put in the Freedmen's Savings Bank. That fall I went to work for a very wealthy lady, Mrs. Charles Green, as laundress. In the spring, Mr. and Mrs. Green went north to Rye Beach, New Hampshire, for the summer. As their cook did not care to go so far from home, I went with them in her place. While there, I won a prize for excellent cooking at

SCHOOLS FOR FORMER SLAVES

After the war many abolitionists worked with the Freedmen's Bureau, a government agency set up to aid and protect the newly freed blacks in the South. One of their first goals was to give the former slaves an education. Schools were set up throughout the Southern states. The teachers, who usually came from the North, encountered many difficulties. White Southerners often snubbed them and refused them room and board. Some teachers were insulted or even beaten and their schoolhouses were set on fire.

Teachers also faced challenges in the classroom. Right after the war, black people moved around a great deal, making it hard for them to attend school regularly. Black children from farm families had to leave school at planting and harvest time to help in the fields. Because their parents could not read or write, many of these children had never even heard of the alphabet. Despite all these problems, the former slaves, both young and old, wanted desperately to learn and worked hard at getting an education.

a fair which the ladies who were summering there held to raise funds to build an Episcopal church. Mrs. Green was one of the energetic workers to make this fair a success; and it was a success in every respect, and a tidy sum was netted.

Through the kindness of Mrs. Barnard, a daughter of ex-Mayor Otis of Boston, I went to Boston in 1874. Soon after I got to Boston, I entered the service of Mr. Thomas Smith's family, on Walnut Avenue, Boston Highlands, where I remained until the death of Mrs. Smith. I next lived with Mrs. Gorham Gray, Beacon Street, where I remained until I was married in 1879 to Russell L. Taylor.

Another Accident at Sea

In 1880 I had another accident at sea. My husband and I started for New York on the steamer *Stonington*. Sometime in the night, the *Narragansett* collided with our boat. I was awakened by the crash. I was in the ladies' cabin. There were about thirty-five or forty others in the cabin. I sprang out of my berth and dressed as quickly as I could. We found the cabin door locked, and two men stood outside and would not let us out. About twenty minutes after, they opened the doors and we went up on deck.

A terrible scene was before us. The *Narragansett* was on fire, in a bright blaze. The water was lighted as far as one could see. The passengers were shrieking, groaning, running about, leaping into the water, panic-stricken. A

A terrible scene was before us. The Narragansett was on fire, in a bright blaze. The water was lighted as far as one could see.

steamer came to our assistance. They put the life rafts off and saved a great many from the burning ship, and picked a number up from the water. A colored man saved his wife and child by giving each a chair and having them jump overboard. These chairs kept them afloat until they were taken aboard by the life raft.

The *Narragansett* was burned to the water's edge. All the passengers were transferred to another steamer and got to New York at 9:30 the next morning. A number of lives were lost in this accident, and the bow of the *Stonington* was badly damaged. I was thankful for my escape, and I have come to the conclusion I shall never have a watery grave.

The Women's Relief Corps

All this time my interest in the boys in blue had not abated. I was still loyal and true, whether they were black or white. My hands have never left undone anything I could do towards their comfort in the twilight of their lives. In 1886 I helped to organize Corps 67, a chapter of the Women's Relief Corps, auxiliary to the G.A.R. (Grand Army of the Republic). It is a very flourishing corps today. I have been Guard, Secretary, Treasurer for three years, and in 1893 I was made President of this corps.

Racism at the Start of the Twentieth Century

Living here in Boston, where the black man is given equal justice, I must say a word on the general treatment of my race, both in the North and South, in this twentieth century. I wonder if our white fellow men realize the true sense or meaning of brotherhood? For two hundred years we had toiled for them. The war of 1861 came and was ended, and we thought our race was forever free from bondage, and that the two races could live in unity with each other. Yet when we read almost every day what is being done to my race by some whites in the South, I sometimes ask, "Was the war in vain? Has it brought freedom, in the full sense of the word, or has it not made our condition more hopeless?"

In this "land of the free" we are burned, tortured, and denied a fair trial. We are murdered for any imaginary wrong conceived in the brain of the Negro-hating white man. There is no redress for us from a government which promised to protect all under its flag. It seems a mystery to me. They say, "One flag, one nation, one country indivisible." Is this true?

Can we say this truthfully when one race is allowed to burn, hang, and inflict the most horrible torture weekly, monthly, on another? No, we cannot sing, "My country, 'tis of thee, sweet land of Liberty"! It is hollow mockery. The Southland laws are all on the side of the white, and they do just as they like to the Negro, whether in the right or not.

I do not uphold my race when they do wrong. They ought to be punished, but the innocent are made to suffer as well as the guilty, and I hope the time will hasten when it will be stopped forever. I may not live to see it, but the time is approaching when the South will again have to repent for the blood it has shed of innocent black men. The South still has a hatred toward the blacks, although there are some true Southern gentlemen left who abhor that hatred, and I hope the day is not far distant when the two races will reside in peace in the Southland.

Real-Life Horrors

I read an article, which said the Confederate Daughters had sent a petition to the managers of the local theaters in Tennessee to prohibit the performance of *Uncle Tom's Cabin*. They claimed it was exaggerated (that is, the treatment of the slaves), and would have a very bad effect on the children who witnessed it. When I was a mere girl, many times I saw thirty or forty men, handcuffed, and as many women and children, come every first Tuesday of each month to the auction blocks.

Do these Confederate Daughters ever send petitions to prohibit the atrocious lynchings and wholesale murdering and torture of the Negro? Do you ever hear of them fearing this would have a bad effect on the children? Which of these two, the drama or the present state of affairs, makes a degrading impression upon the minds of our young generation? In my opinion it is not *Uncle Tom's Cabin,* but it should be the one that has caused the world to cry "Shame!" It does not seem as if our land is yet civilized.

A Visit to Louisiana

On February 3, 1898, I was called to Shreveport, Louisiana, to the bedside of my son, who was very ill. He was touring with Nickens and Company [an acting troupe], with *The Lion's Bride,* when he fell ill, and had been ill two weeks when they sent for me. I tried to have him brought home to Boston, but they could not send him, as he was not able to sit and ride this long distance. So on the sixth of February I left Boston to go to him. I reached Cincinnati on the eighth, where I took the train for the South.

Before I got my train, I asked a white man standing nearby what car I should take. "Take that one," he said, pointing. "But that is a smoking car!" "Well," he replied, "that is the car for colored people." I went to this car, and on entering it, all my courage failed me. I have ridden in many coaches, but I was never in such as these. The car was dirty and unpleasant. I wanted to return home again,

"That is the car for colored people."

but when I thought of my sick boy, I said, "Well, others ride in these cars and I must do likewise." I tried to be resigned, for I wanted to reach my boy, as I did not know whether I should find him alive.

I arrived in Chattanooga, Tennessee, at eight o'clock in the evening, where the porter took my baggage to the train which was to leave for Marion, Mississippi. Soon after I was seated, just before the train pulled out, two tall men with slouch hats walked through the car, and on through the train. Finally they came back to our car and, stopping at my seat, said, "Where are those men who came in with you?" I did not know to whom they were speaking, as there was another woman in the car, so I made no reply. Again they asked me, standing directly in front of my seat, "Where are those men who came in with you?"

"Are you speaking to me?" I said.

"Yes," they said.

"I have not seen any men," I replied.

They looked at me a moment, and one of them asked where I was from. I told him Boston. He hesitated a minute and walked out of our car to the other car.

When the conductor came around, I told him what these men had said, and asked him if they allowed persons to enter the car and insult passengers. He only smiled. Later, when the porter came in, I mentioned it to him. He said, "Lady, I see you do not belong here. Where are you from?" I told him. He said, "I have often heard of Massachusetts. I want to see that place."

"Yes!" I said. "You can ride there on the cars, and no person would be allowed to speak to you as those men did to me." He explained that those men were constables. "That is the way they do here. Each morning you can hear of some Negro being lynched." On seeing my surprise, he said, "Oh, that is nothing. It is done all the time. We have no rights here. I have been on this road for fifteen years and have seen some terrible things." He wanted to know what I was doing down there, and I told him it was only the illness of my son that brought me there.

"No Mercy to Negroes"

I got to Marion, Mississippi, at two o'clock in the morning, arrived at Vicksburg at noon, and at Shreveport about eight o'clock in the evening. I found my son just recovering from a severe hemorrhage. He was very anxious to come home, and I tried to secure a berth for him on a sleeper train, but they would not sell me one, and he was not strong enough to travel otherwise. If I could only have gotten him to Cincinnati, I might have brought him home. As I could not, I was forced to let him remain where he was. It seemed very hard, when his father fought to protect the Union and our flag, and yet his boy was denied a berth to carry him home to die, because he was a Negro.

In Shreveport a man was murdered in cold blood for nothing. He was a colored man and a "porter" in a store. A clerk in the store had left his umbrella at home. It had begun to rain when he started for home, and on looking for the umbrella he could not, of course, find it. He asked the porter if he had seen it. He said no, he had not.

"You answer very saucy," said the clerk, and drawing his revolver, he shot the colored man dead. The clerk was taken up the street to an office, where he was placed under one thousand dollars bond for his appearance and released. That was the end of the case. I was surprised at this, but I was told by several white and colored persons that it was a common occurrence; the persons were never punished if they were white, but no mercy was shown to Negroes.

I met several comrades, white and colored, in Shreveport, and noticed that the colored comrades did not wear their buttons [from the Union army]. I asked one of them why this was, and was told that if they wore the buttons, they could not get work. Still, some would wear their buttons in spite of the feeling against it.

We Ask for Justice!

After the death of my son, while on my way back to Boston, I came to Clarksdale, one of the stations on the road from Vicksburg. There, I saw a man hanged. It was a terrible sight, and I felt alarmed for my own safety down there. When I reached Memphis, I found conditions of travel much better. The people were mostly Western and Northern here. The cars were nice, but separate for colored persons until we reached the Ohio River. Then the door was opened and the porter passed through, saying, "The Ohio River! Change to the other car."

I thought, What does he mean? We have been riding all this distance in separate cars, and now we are all to sit together? It certainly seemed a peculiar arrangement.

While in Shreveport, I had visited ex-Senator Harper's house. He is a colored man and owns a large business block, besides a fine residence on Cado Street and several good building lots. Another family, the Pages, living on the same street, were quite wealthy. A large number of colored families owned their homes, and were industrious, refined people. If they were only allowed justice, the South would be the only place for our people to live.

We are similar to the children of Israel, who, after many weary years in bondage, were led into that land of promise, to thrive and be forever free from persecution.

What a wonderful revolution! In 1861 the Southern papers were full of advertisements for "slaves," but now, despite all the hindrances and "race problems," my people are striving for the standard of all other races born free in the sight of God. In a number of instances they have succeeded. Justice we ask, to be citizens of these United States, where so many of our people have shed their blood with their white comrades, that the Stars and Stripes should never be polluted.

The End

Editor's Note

The text in this book has been abridged from Susie King Taylor's self-published autobiography *Reminiscences of My Life in Camp with the 33d United States Colored Troops Late 1st S.C. Volunteers.* The book came out in 1902, thirty-seven years after the end of the Civil War. In editing Susie's work, I have modernized spellings, capitalization, and punctuation, and sometimes compressed her long and ornate sentences. Occasionally I have made small changes for the sake of clarity. Otherwise, the wording throughout is Susie's.

Glossary

abhor despise

abolitionists Americans, mostly from the North, who wanted to end slavery

auxiliary an organization that works as a branch of a larger group

berth a bed or place to sleep on a train or ship

bounty a payment or reward given by the government

cartridge a case holding gunpowder and bullets, for loading into a rifle

cast away left adrift at sea after a shipwreck

cavalry the part of an army that fights on horseback

Confederates the people of the Southern states that seceded from the Union

convent a residence for nuns, which may include a school for girls

cordial friendly, warm

effects possessions

Emancipation Proclamation President Lincoln's act that freed all the slaves in the Confederate states

evacuate to leave a place

furlough a leave of absence for a soldier

hardtack an unsalted hard biscuit

hemorrhage heavy bleeding

Ku Klux Klan a secret organization of white men
organized after the Civil War to terrorize and
intimidate African Americans, Jews, and other
minority groups

laurel an evergreen shrub with white or pink flowers

lynchings killings by a mob, usually by hanging

mess pan cooking pan

molest disturb, annoy

mustered out discharged from the service

non-commissioned officers lower-ranking officers
appointed from among the enlisted men

plantation a large farm estate

quartermaster an army officer who provides clothing
and other supplies to the troops

ramparts a protective barrier before a fort

redress compensation for a wrong or loss

sassafras a tree whose dried root bark was used for tea,
medicine, and flavoring

scourge a cause of widespread suffering

sharecroppers farmers who work someone else's land
in return for a share of the crops

slave law the Georgia Slave Codes of 1848, which
included severe penalties for slaves who committed a
variety of minor and major offenses

smallpox a disease that causes fever and skin eruptions
and is sometimes fatal

staunch faithful

stockades enclosures for prisoners

tapping cutting in on a line, such as a telegraph or
phone line, to get information

Uncle Tom's Cabin a novel by Harriet Beecher Stowe
that dramatized the mistreatment of slaves; also a
play based on the book

Yankees Northerners

To Learn More about the Civil War and Reconstruction

Books

Nonfiction

Chang, Ina. *A Separate Battle: Women and the Civil War.* New York: Lodestar Books, 1991.

Gay, Kathlyn, and Martin Gay. *Civil War.* New York: Twenty-First Century Books, 1995.

Lester, Julius. *To Be a Slave.* New York: Dial Books, 1998.

McConnell, Jane Tompkins. *Cornelia, the Story of a Civil War Nurse.* New York: Crowell, 1959.

McKissack, Patricia C., and Fredrick L. McKissack. *Christmas in the Big House, Christmas in the Quarters.* New York: Scholastic, 1994.

Murphy, Jim. *The Boys' War: Confederate and Union Soldiers Talk about the Civil War.* New York: Clarion Books, 1990.

Ray, Delia. *A Nation Torn: The Story of How the Civil War Began.* New York: Lodestar Books/Dutton, 1990.

Schomp, Virginia. *Letters from the Homefront: The Civil War.* New York: Benchmark Books, 2002.

Fiction

Hansen, Joyce. *I Thought My Soul Would Rise and Fly: The Diary of Patsy, a Freed Girl.* New York: Scholastic, 1997.

Hesse, Karen. *A Light in the Storm: The Civil War Diary of Amelia Martin.* New York: Scholastic, 1999.

Nixon, Joan Lowery. *A Dangerous Promise.* New York: Delacorte, 1994.

Paulsen, Gary. *Soldier's Heart: A Novel of the Civil War.* New York: Delacorte Press, 1998.

Websites*

Slave narratives from the Federal Writers' Project, 1936–1938
http://lcweb2.loc.gov/ammem/snhtml/

Women of the American Civil War
www.americancivilwar.com/women/women.html

Photos of Civil War soldiers, generals, camps
http://memory.loc.gov/ammem/cwphtml/cwphome.html

*Websites change from time to time. For additional on-line information, check with the media specialist at your local library.

Places To Visit

Andersonville National Historic Site, 496 Cemetery Road, Andersonville, GA 31711
The historic prison site, the National Prisoner of War Museum

Fort Pulaski National Monument, P.O. Box 30757, U.S. Highway 80 East, Savannah, GA 31410
The historic site and exhibits of the fort's history

Fort Sumter National Monument, 1214 Middle Street, Sullivan's Island, SC 29482
The fort, plus a museum and shop

Index

Page numbers for illustrations are in **boldface.**

About the Editor

From the time she was in elementary school, Margaret Gay Malone has loved American history, the Civil War being one of her favorite eras. Reading about Susie King Taylor, she admired her bravery, not only during the war, but also after, when she set out on her own.

Ms. Malone, while pursuing a career in public relations, has written eight books, seven of them for children. She lives in a small town on Long Island with her husband, Tom, a dog, and two cats.

DATE DUE

Printed
in USA